DUES FOR THE REPOSE

soft strings, sharp concord,
the legend of my sensibilities
written

DUES FOR THE REPOSE
FROM WORDS MUCH LIKE POETRY

Urban Centigrade*
751 East 161 Street, Apt. 7A
Bronx, NY 10456
www.urbancentigrade.com
Email: wamuhu.mwaura@urbancentigrade.com

Urban Centigrade* logos are proprietary and copyright protected.
Designed by Antony Kamau.

Cover image: Lotus flower plant by Karen Arnold (Public Domain). Floral pattern: (Public Domain). Background with flowers by Larisa Koshkina. Dharma wheel licensed under the Attribution-ShareAlike 3.0 Unported (CC BY-SA 3.0). Celtic Knot: (Public domain). Embedded image links may change and/or may no longer be valid from date of publication of this work. Lettering and interior design by Wamuhu Mwaura.

Author photograph by Jose Figueroa.
Copyright © 2013 Jose Figueroa

Ordering Information, quantity sales:

Special discounts are available on quantity purchases by individuals, small businesses, and localized retailers. For details, contact the publisher at the address above. Orders by U.S. trade bookstores and wholesalers, please contact publisher via e-mail above.

ISBN: 978-0-9903043-0-2

Printed in the United States of America

DUES FOR THE REPOSE
FROM WORDS MUCH LIKE POETRY

POETIC WORKS BY

WAMUHU MWAURA

URBAN
centigrade
URBAN CENTIGRADE®
NEW YORK

AUTHOR'S NOTE:

Dear Reader,

At nine, I self-published my first work, a superhero epic titled *Wrath of the Red Bird* which totaled no more than 4 pages of loose-leaf, stapled together paper.

In the spring of 2007, I received my first publication by an online literary magazine. That publication spurred me to create a poetry blog, *Words Much Like Poetry*, which was an exercise in courage. My poetry is extremely personal in nature, you see—an exorcism of roiling thoughts, mercurial emotions, of joy and hurt and heartache (most especially heartache). But, "Courage is the price that life exacts for granting peace," (Amelia Earhart).

Blogging offered the barest beginnings of peace where my writing is concerned, and, in finding peace, I found the strength to reach for a new goal.

A yet again self-published work under my recently registered trademark, *Dues for the Repose, From Words Much Like Poetry*, is the culmination of five years of little bits of betrayal—somewhat fantastical, mostly autobiographical, it is a journey through various mythologies into the concrete depths of my spirituality, and even further into the yawning caverns of vivid memory in a quest to ascertain the boundaries of my self-efficacy.

Sincerely,
Wamuhu Mwaura
CEO and Editor-in-Chief, Urban Centigrade®

For Jack.
You were the first to believe.

CONTENTS
f

TERRENE AND THE OLD MOON

At the inception,
the terrestrial sphere lay bare beneath the orb of night,
and enamored of her fawning substance
Old Moon skimmed a greeting,
an unrefined glance—
his extremities cavorted over her mainstays,
the visceral curvature of her mean,
the splay of the sophisticate,
and Terrene's sleek quarter—
to brace the wake of this vale's cusp.

In elemental persuasion,
Old Moon urged Terrene,
enticing her high in contrast to his side,
and when she sang low at the prospect,
Old Moon obliged
settling the champion of his adamant construction
at the gateway of Terrene's stormy essence.

A purposeful advance and Old Moon had Terrene
bowing in opposition. Inhaling sharply,
he exalted at the semblance of Terrene,
and burgeoning, followed his champion
into a series of restricted exchanges.

Shortly, perception became the basis of existence,
buffeting Old Moon with its material compulsions,
and Terrene could only cleave herself unto him,
lithesome vocalizations fissuring into the heavens.

Vitality frayed, as fleet as Old Moon's own,
she solicited a persistent endearment,
for their obligation had neared its original end.

Her planes began to seize, drawing forth creation,
and Terrene soared into profligacy,
all the while simperingly regarding the beatific.

EVE'S LACKING

They met in years still tender—
days so long buried in the passage of time
it seems that they walked in the newest of light.

Upon continents that knew no division,
the Greater Force molded mountains
as they walked in the newest of light

alongside rivers of fire.
Though, if asked, that Eve of gentle desire—
met in years still tender,

days long buried in the passage of time—
would have scoffed at the beasts of the realm
and told them in terms lacking no uncertainty

that knowledge was hers, and no fruit, forbidden or otherwise,
could convey upon her any further wisdom—
if only in years still tender

Lilith had intervened, but she abandoned Eden
to Adam and the Fall; to Earth she became the night,
where she met Samael in years still tender—
and they walked new in the absence of light.

CIRCUIT OF STRENGTH FOR THE NEEDFUL FORM

Obscurity, the will of Gaea reaches into Hydros,
and even the Ourea cease to matter as you stretch
your well-modulated voice and ask quietly of me,

"What do you long for?"

Face burning brightly, a star gone nova,
I want to say, "I long to make of my body a haven.
Nestle inside of me and take your respite."

Instead, I utter words of a more prudent nature.

"Forgive me, but the complexity of my emotions,
which lurk beneath a wizened veneer,
became, as days and weeks and years disappeared into

Ananke the Inevitable, difficult to put sensibly into words—

Disastrous mistress, she forges her way ever forward,
shoulders rigid, serpentine head aloft,
deaf ear turned to every desperate plea that she halt,

too far apart for even the most ambitious of bridges

                    to span. That fear
kept my feelings from lacking proper definition,
kept them as particles of dust, lambent upon

destiny's continually changing breeze."

You return, "Time is no longer a wretched whore.
Now, her headlong flight through long, soft hours of night,
and bright, incandescent days, is a thing to be rejoiced.

She speeds us along

toward that moment when you will become once more
solid warmth, tender love. And, too, that which you cannot
in the turbulence of your cynicism say, will be enticed to spill

honeyed from your lips by the fine tremors that course

along the limbs I wrap tightly,
in an unending circuit of strength,
about your needful form."

What Needs Be Overcome

This courtship of ours is tenuous,
a frail reassertion, at best,
of my capability to feel emotions
I've long thought of as a realm from which I'd been exiled.

Into this crucial measure,
Ninhursag of the land of civilized kings
raises mountain and rolling hill as interruption,
while Amathaounta of the Elamites,
beckons the brash to venture into her deep.
See you Ashima atop Shomron,
guiding time and fortune both?
Unalterable course plotted,
she makes of us misanthropes, whose ill intents
are borne toward the roseate.

And that withered woman wisdom,
who was Ninkarrak to the Assyrians
and Ninsu-Utud to the Akkadians,
who gains us patiently her teachings,
reminding us with merciless fondness,
that one can no more dwell in ignorance
of the ways of mortal mankind,
than one can dwell in endless night—
for withered woman wisdom is much like An,
the lustrous sun, the light of truth that nourishes our souls,

furnishing a most improbable chance
to at last rid ourselves of Zaltu—

for she, too, needs be overcome—
strife, that malaise of the spirit,
that cunning creature known well as heartache.

MORTAR AND BRICKS

It was more than a late summer romance,
I pressed closed the hole in your heart,
a rough shod patch I bore into this world—
the angels confessed
I would be in need one day.

In September of *that* year, I betrayed you.
October found forgiveness a new home,
but by January, I hadn't seen you in weeks.
When I did, you bundled me into a rocket
and launched me at the eternal sky—
I landed somewhere between Castor and Pollux.
Merry gentleman boys that they were,
I eventually lost my ability to distinguish them
and nicknamed them the Gemini man.
Hmph! before long Jason bade him marry me.
So, the Argo made port in the western province
of the home where my soul still unwillingly resides;
that was late March.
While there a faithful man repeated my cue,
from then one became my number.

An ancient age or a few years passed,
by then the Argo had sailed,
dust trails the only evidence it ever existed.
My family summoned me and expectantly,
I packed lightly—the little pieces of myself
I couldn't do without. The Gemini man
I surrendered.

My kin, a little lasting embrace.

Once released from their fold,
I bought myself a river and sang the blues at its side.
A Virgin strolling by heard my song
and swayed well to the rhythm.
Together, we danced.
But soon, that less than pure vestal tired,
for
in my land, sorrow rains down as thick as honey,
and
hopes, ambitions, hell even dreams are cloying.
He trilled gleefully to the meadowlark
perched upon the withered stump of the once Life Tree.
Just as blithely, the imp spread its wings,
casting me in shadow.

Thirteen years have passed since our late summer love.
I wonder if you've torn down the mortar and bricks I laid.
If so, cracked and broken as they might be,
can I borrow them?

NEW YORK CITY BLUES

My cobalt city, my indigo restraint,
I thought to grow my wings here,

to hone each gallant feather upon the flustering streets,
the agitated walkways that run several countries and cultures
        deep,

I did not expect an aviary to bound out of the metropolis,
to spring closed and laud my seizure,

but it has, but it did.

I've gauged the reach it would take to appropriate my license,
the unending azure sky needs only half as many strides to cross,

and the good auspices have gone calling on others.
Come then defeat and take their place,

let our association begin,
turn me 'round the city's bend,

tap me in Celtic fashion at the entrance to the Empire State,
roam with me the Botanical Gardens and that place, Central
        Park,

mourn, also, the ground that numbers nil.

Hide from me though, my Lady Liberty,
for sight of her would surely persuade me to shed my winter skins,

to stand taller as the trees do when the birds return their
        weight,
to quiet the strums of the guitar blues

and sway instead to the rhythm of unseen drums,
marching me along to battle once more

for the immunity of flight, the prerogative to soar.

THE INDIGENT STATE

At highest hilltop, I pause world-worn bones
and gaze below at the indigent state,
where, in beggarly raiment, I reside.

A sullying fate, this circumstance impoverishment,
from which there seems no evasion—
insipid tale, the daily warfare of tenement life, soar,
stentorian dimensions, no quiet remonstration,
these querulous folk refuse soft sighers here.

I would shield my ears if I could, an escutcheon depicting
hands cupped in reverent imitation of the sea-keeper shell,
a maiden listening to the whirl of her own blood ocean,
thinking of the worth long denied her, of staple humility.

Form breaks and my knees land jarringly
upon the gradually changeable earth.
I make no sound, though my eyes are now fountains
Which

c
a
s
c
a
d
e

salt ridden jets

onto the well-traveled curvatures below.
No, I dare not waste breath to make testimonials—
baleful happenings long consummated—
for the grandiose fledged circles above
and in this act, this stereotypical urban tragedy,
I finally speak.

"Phoenix of renewal,
with your flames bathe clean
this defective manifestation, broken of
a more knowledgeable mold, into ash, then dust,
then call forth the four winds, scatter me across the heavens,
where vindication might find me and cast me yet again into
the fire, into continued trial for the wealth of a sprawl filled
to the brim with fat years constructed of palmy days,
towering windfalls, and the bounteous returns
of my rightful
gains."

Muted Noises

It was never my intent to give silence sovereignty,
dominion over my kingdom hub,
nor to gather self-pity and lay it about

a moat to the castle of my heart.
I assigned no consequence to the betrayal—
gather self-pity and lay it about

majestic tower rooms, placed at loving heights
distinctly for solace, a highness's plight;
silent sovereignty, it was never my intent to give

dominion over my kingdom hub
to the strain of stinting love;—
trials best told in the sullen aftermath,

the sound of their relation
nothing more than muted noises.
Never to give silence sovereignty was my intent,

but I am a flawed animal, fallible and comforted
by the customs which define me:
give silence sovereignty, with the intent
to gather self-pity and lay it about.

HUMAN NATURE

I.

I've often been told that my eyes speak volumes,
and all the thoughts and emotions that wander aimlessly
through the dimly lit corridors of my spirit self

are written plainly for those with the ability to translate them
from whatever ancient language is spoken by the soul.
Through the dimly lit corridors of my spirit self

fear of sensitives summons those empaths who are privy
to that which I, by no willing intention, telegraph. Pity
that I've often been told my eyes speak volumes,

and all the thoughts and emotions that wander aimlessly,
lurking the deepest recesses of my basis—
a barely contained beast, a monstrous part of me,

vengeful incarnation, worshiper of malevolence,
creep forward from your iniquitous home!
I've often been told that my eyes speak volumes

when my baser and more wrathful passions burn brightest,
a tale of discovery to impart the understanding,
that often my eyes speak volumes, resounding
through the dimly lit corridors of my spirit self.

II.

At day's end, upon the lonely stretch, sweat soaked, heaving,
teeth clenched against the banshee like screams
that fill my chords to the brim,

my eyes, o curtain less panes of tempered glass,
are shut. For if by some mischance
I fill my chords to the brim,

o sensitive, cower when you peer into me
in the nighttime hours, piercing the suspended obscurity
that lies upon the lonely stretch, sweat soaked, heaving,

teeth clenched against the banshee like screams,
the struggle at its fiercest, a leech to the potent convictions
that have wielded their legend across all vitality—

Faith!—for the malignant spawn festers,
hold and further dissuade affinity, embrace not
the lonely stretch, sweat soaked, heaving,

read gently the nature of temporal dwellers,
fall hesitantly into the bleak of the river despair.
Lay then upon the lonely stretch, sweat soaked, heaving,
your chords filled to the brim with prayer.

THE STAINED EARTH

The early end to days has fled,
        dusk and twilight bide their time,
seizing into the new stretch of light
        bird song and the merriment of the young of our flock.

The sounds play a lucid harmony
        to the screaming wails that follow violence.
I bend my ear closer to my makeshift dwelling,
        huddling inside its blank walls, all the while straining
against the pull of a new generation's hands,

they seek an outlet in the warmth I fear to accommodate,
        they haven't the persuasion I've gained.
In enviable innocence,
        shadowed walk-ins, with their hung cargo,

folded denim wear, and stacked foot coverings,
        hide monsters of fairy tale lore,
not the thoroughfares with their lurking ills,
        where thunder rolls like luminous ire in the distance—

I wish it would become a downpour,
        hard, pelting drops, a genesis
that would flood creation and revivify it.
        But that is mere hope.

Discontent has left a lurid smear on its surface—
        wretched fiend, humanity; a devil-may-care criminal
come in search of a concert with good fortune.

Treble clef; C minor into major at four-four time;

quickening it at the motif, a harrowing fugue;
    decrescendo, coda, conclude the spanning movement,
and what stunning release that final token,
    a relief from the unending conflict—mortal men

seem intent upon a forceful return to paradise,
    so many souls, they weigh down the vault of heaven,
delving the firmament into the fertile soil, seeding;
    without repent, the belly of the Great Mother becomes the pit.

THE WEIGHT OF WATER

obstructions forged,
altercations with serrated edges;

cannikins, which wield words much like poetry,
pay homage to the scars that delineate my face,

from lachryma (failed time and again in their attempt
to deluge my barriers, to wreak their portent),

wishes stream upward, imploring for days sunny,

abject refusals to assign the weight of that water significance,
though fearsome it may be—mountains sturdier than I have
          given way,

formed canyons to channel it, so that the world's grief
might stream steadily into Poseidon's cherished hold—

perhaps a day will come when that substance, held back,
finds its merry way around hindrances, as the lymphate is wont to
          do

until then, I shall drown only in the words granted leave
to express that which I have denied license.

SPEAK THE GENTLE FLICKER

The meadowlark peers down from its gracious perch
upon the withered stump of the once Life Tree,
its displeasure has cast ills as long as memory has served.

The mark I assigned my penury warbles, a flute like call—
it refuses to be daunted by that holy wood—
displeasure, cast ills, long memory serve

to speak to the gentle flicker of my pride,
"*Sing a song of salvation, an ode to the rightful guide—*"
From its perch, the meadowlark peers down

at the withered stump of the once Life Tree.
Its manifesto having taken umbrage with that pitiable patch,
the meadowlark sneers at its gracious perch.

I pull closer, willfully at arms, obdurate while I shiver.
"Do you so despise me? I ask only honored and saintly woes,"
again the meadowlark, as it peers at me.

I say, "I am not so tenderhearted as you perceive, but for the sake
of that which gambles upon my form, I bend to your will."
The meadowlark peers down at me from its gracious perch,
its pleasure, to cast ills 'til long memory serves.

TOSS UP

I. SON

He's too close, Carol Anne might swallow him whole
for a play date in the white noise flickering
in electronic diatribe from the television screen.
He spares me a laughing glance when I plead my case
and acquits me of being maudlin every time I drink in

the difference nine years can make.

He's a sapling—limbs long and bare, fresh—
so I tend him, combing newspaper shreds into the fertile soil
about his roots to keep the creepers from wasting
what cleverness might have been woven into his bark.
He'll walk tall when he's ready; like Treebeard,

he cannot be rushed into heroics for some silly status in legend,

and certainly not while shot up full of arrows
that bleed poison into his heightened awareness
just to keep him grounded in logic that hardly equates;
this patchwork skin birthed him,
and never you mind the anguish I suffered

in wait of three little words:

I love you,
I love you, I love you,
I love you

he says now 'til I've had enough, 'til my heart collapses
for how tight he's wrapped his consequence around it;

how can any one woman survive him?

II. Daughter

It's a toss-up who I love more; I still see her
little fist settled against my full breast—
she suckled longer and I eventually realized
it was more for my comfort than for her sustenance;
my nipples still ache for the hard bite of tiny teeth,

but she is no longer small,

the crook of my arm can no longer hold her length,
and the skin of her knees, once as soft as the rest of her,
is weathered—first by the harsh, constant drag
of carpet fibers against it and now by the kind of rough play
I engaged in when I was her age, trying to prove

that I was just as tough as the boys.

I want to tell her everything I've learned
but I'm afraid she won't believe, some tales
are just too fantastic to be told, they have to be lived.
This though, I'll say because it's the most obvious truth,
life is a contradiction, but I won't even try to explain

how in light there waits darkness,

and in the darkest of times, upon the most troubled
of paths, there waits real love, the realization of everything
that you dream, because nothing that is not earned,
not paid for with some sort of sacrifice, whether it be
time or ambition or innocence, is worth calling yours.

I smile at daughter lovingly, for she is mine.

DEPTHS OF A DUAL FACETED MIND'S EYE

Remembrances, still water glass,
well preserved faculty;

upon this play visions—

the fragmented depths of a dual faceted mind's eye—
acts of an eagerly sought-after awakening,

longing given character and speech.

Grim brush strokes, predictable disenchantment,
discordant tones astray under moonless night,

communion solely meant, a snare—

six and twenty years it took the meadowlark to confide
aggrieved remembrances etched on still water glass,

the fragmented depths of a dual faceted mind's eye.

THE SUNDAY USUAL

The pots are black, again;
>   you... *cooked.*
I smelled the burn halfway,
>   when I mentioned it, you smirked,

I shrugged, inwardly sighed,
>   three a.m. would find me tossing from hunger.
We sit to eat. I pick, you devour,
>   our wingless cherubs turn away their faces

from the spoons that I aim at their rosy mouths.
>   We argue, you walk out.
I don't want you to return—
>   you can't admit to your mistakes,

I can't admit I don't love you.
>   Perhaps once, I was enthralled.
You were striking, with eyes like sun-fired amber
>   that refused to douse their inner flame.

I, have been made ugly
>   by my woe. Go
away, and let me fade,
>   though there will remain

within these walls, echoes of your presence,
>   in your children—
the particular round of their faces,
>   their hawk like noses,

and eyebrows which slash dramatically
> over eyes as brilliant as yours.
If this is an end,
> I won't try intimacy again,

it requires too much;
> I have nothing left to give.
Shreds are all that exist
> of the once whole heart I possessed—

the largest scraps belong to my children,
> and to a bright star in the distant heavens
I cannot help but love—
> still, give it back,

whole, but for the pieces
> my earthbound miracles claim,
only them and me,
> a little trilogy of misery.

I am shackled to poverty.
> it weighs my steps, makes of me a wretch
and keeps the profession, "I hate you!"
> sealed behind my withered lips.

The locks turn, playing like strains,
> a haunting piece in the depths of my soul.
Mouth tight, eyes averted,
> I welcome you back.

CONTENT ME, IF YOU WOULD

An *a capella* of sinful verse sounds
to serenade this conference of familiar strangers,
and, o, how my veins thrill to those gospel truths
hummed along elicited receptors,
sung to consecrated need,
sweet, sweet substance,
which centers upon a refined hollow,
wept materiality.

In offer of respite from the steep incline,
the torturous agitation,
you lay upon me a coarse vernacular,
a language with which I am knowledgeable,
though your dialect and diction, are—
prior to this engagement—woefully unknown;
and further, in search of the spare,
you make complete my elegant casing,
a superficial extent you serve well
with a falchion of sainted yearning.

Thus, we arrive at the beginning of wonder,
privity and insight, approval and commendation;
rhythm follows, the chant of the possession,
the murmur of the yield,
a searing *tango criollo*,
"that emptiness to which we put movement"[1]
and into that bargain, come the various catastrophes.

Firstly, the encroaching tide,

[1]Carlos Gavito (b. 1942 – d. 2005)

a flood sensationally hued,
waters channeled of a soft parting;
secondly, the shift of the tectonic,
the lines of fault stemming of a staggered and quaking heart,
thirdly, the celestial burn, the zenith of the fueled core,
and lastly, o at last, the coveted return and its penurious
successor,
blessed surcease, hallowed cessation.

3 A.M. LAMENT

Once again, in for a share, a rapacious interlude,
and sated for a spell, the perpetual season of my anger
lies disrupted.

With the conclusion of our rare distraction,
there is now within you a sense of righteous dominance,
an assumption that I have yielded to your brand,
to your careless love,
and that guilt has no residence
in the streets of your conscience.

But remorse ought have a comfortable shelter,
an extravagant domicile in the vicinity of your soul,
for the era of

my self-abasement—
a frigid, unending winter,
calculable years—

was began
by the first strike you laid
upon the softly rounded curve of my cheek.
O curse the inanity of my sense of judgment;
curse my misguided faith, the bonding of the human form,
I knew, I knew!

At the commencement of the affair,
there was to you a savageness,
temper flashes made of your eyes a moisture bereft plain

whereupon wildfires spread and blaze intensely,
but I thought, too, that you were civil enough
to reign in your violent tendencies,
thought there was to be found a measure,
some esteem for those fairer, often weaker
in the sense of the physical

(*I reasoned that since woman, as I, gave birth to you,*
endured for you the terrible onslaught, the labor,
tending you to her breast and wasting herself to sustain you...)

         A tear
             coasts
                  a salty path,

staining my originally insulted, and continually
offended presumption. I pull closer
            the sackcloth and the ashes
my sheets and bedspread have become.

They mourn with me the extent of my naiveté.
For though the glacial fury has descended and restarted whatever
timepiece tracks the course, my enduring ire,
the hour of elegy is done.
Three a.m. is now four, time to sleep.

The babes will wake and need me,
or whatever pathetic creature it is that rises,
angry and drawn from the nightly lament,
to a sad existence that is more than in her power
to change.

WASTELAND DREAMS

Upon the Shoes of Swiftness, I jaunt down Inachus,
perhaps in reverie, as Arachne weaves a stunted tapestry
upon the wall and floor—gloomy, bitter, tragic spun—
and I am Pallas Athene, a woman of infinite promise
beleaguered by creation; I suffer the strain of consciousness,
I haven't the choice, like that woman turned spider
thoughts of self-imposed death swirled gracelessly

beneath still waters, a facade; I captured her.

Near Joppa, guarded by a monster of the Earthshaker's lending,
I left her chained without hope—for Perseus is long dead,
abandoned to oblivion by the fickle beliefs of men—
that wounded, angry child I can never again be;
I am distanced by the gashes shorn into my flesh,
riving that ever-fixed the consort, the son by Orhpic hymn,
the personification of delight, a glance into my womb.

I sought to reason with her once, the guilt overwhelming.

The Tamer of Horses soothed his beast, beckoning it to his side,
and I scaled embellished links into bygone years, where
her rages flew like lightning hurled by the Cloudgatherer
toward Titans both real and imagined, "The progenitor!
He suffocates," her most prevalent cry,
and at my approach, she turned to me in coy petulance—
"One day you will join me here;

another comes to take your place."

I trembled then recalled a defiant nature—
though swallowed whole by misery, out of fear perhaps,
like the Oceanid who was Wisdom before me, I find myself fully
      armed,
incapable of being a nymph who owes the world nothing more
than the grace of her beauty. I am weighted down
by that which seems my constant and faithful companion.
She has never failed nor abandoned me.

The woe love brings.

Misery, you cherish me. So well kept
in your heavy shadow, I became a desolate creature,
a floundering wasteland of precious dreams,
where fools and children dwell. Wretched and frivolous,
I was abundantly shallow and invoked you—incited
your presence to find that which I ofttimes required

to accept the silent shambles, the dark abyss, life.

O misery, sweet misery, for the apathy which lies
in the harvest of your content, I devote myself so cruelly,
but you will relinquish claim when the Indigent State
is overrun by The Great Feats, and a new self is born.
"Yes," the acknowledgment, "I, too, shall be bound
in chains whose links are formed by triumph over vicissitude.
Yes," in relief I smiled and, to my former self, conveyed,

"I eagerly await that exchange."

WHEN ANGELS LENT US AUDIENCE

Who wears such shoes, that every step trodden
creaks the tile which sullies the bare cement?
When did my out step begin to weigh so heavily?

I was as silent as ether once, a mere shadow
the most ponderous burden upon my barest self;
when did my out step begin to weigh so heavily?

It once reached tenebrous tendrils to touch wailing souls
nearby—brethren long and long ago acquainted,
who wore such shoes that every step trodden

creaked the tile which sullied the bare cement—
their inner stations tuned to mine,
such melodies our fettered souls would sing,

harmonies grander than Friedrich's hymn,
more tranquil than Françios's march.
Such shoes, that with every step trodden

angels lent us audience, only to abandon us
when our rap sheet of sons and sins ran askance.
Damn these shoes. For with every step trodden,
my out step weighs so heavily.

THE IMMORTALITY OF INTIMATES RECONCILED

I think on intimates, friends well remembered in study,
      and wistful longings begin to nag at my spirit,
they displace the usual lines etched upon my face,
      amounting it to a solemn landscape of woe
for the solitude we wear close to our hearts,
      like cavaliers chain mail and suit of armor
in the way it weighs upon the form,
      sinking us deep into the quagmire loneliness.

I think on the way me and my intimates,
      on those ever rarer occasions of desperation
for that which is much needed but singularly found,
      stretch out to one another arms that tremble
from the exhaustion of carrying individual hindrances
      and touch fingers, in reconciling manner,
across the erstwhile distance of our parallel lives.
      I think on the events that shaped us

and that which drives us even now,
      the seeds of our aspirations which we have sown
and seeking to make fruitful, we tend them
      in the way of gardeners as they begin to grow,
nurturing them as they begin to bloom.
      In each tender bud, I see the prospective for greatness
that lies with the realization of our goals
      and I weep for the endless universe of possibilities

that was secured us by those willing to trade blessed life
      for equality and freedom.

Now, we can be as the empires and the conquerors,
      the poets, the playwrights, the sculptors, the painters,
the inventors and the explorers,
      we can be as ill-forgotten as they,
a mighty root in our tree of known kindred
      and not merely a withering branch.

But I wonder still if I have the right of it,
      or if perhaps I seek nothing more
than a method of explaining away
      my demented longing for the immortality
which comes of great feats and lasts us
      through the ages, kept alive
by those descended of us, by those who speak of us
      until time immemorial.

ATONEMENT

A shade, once tucked into opaque retreats,
into shameful recall, gathers before me.
About him eddies brume, suspending the odyssey,
the existent—that stolen doorway in the corridors of time
which arrives me at the misdeeds of my youth.

And the figure, now the actuality of an intimate,
an agate, crafted into a likening perception,
yet dissimilar in embodiment, though cherished
through dividing lengths, expanses both briny and ...
continuously, he looks coldly upon me.

"Within the clouded past, lie occurrences
approximate to crimes, principally the refute
of the morality engaged upon you from infancy,
indulgences that consumed your inner resplendence,
and compensated your central core

with a disbursement of darkness."
So confronted, with the backlash of a broken character,
the vengeance wreaked upon virtuous personages,
I kneel upon the crystal akin sand, which bites deep
into intentions no longer used to such given praises,

and to extinction and aggregate, say
"The comportment I affected in the generations since
the vagary of my minority,
has done little to find me solace,
no consolation, no dependable release,

all that has been accomplished is the spawning
of dissension within my vital force.
I beg you tell me, how then do I find atonement,
when I have become so estranged from the certitudes
that were once eminently comparable to typical matters?"

THE HERETIC IN VARIED FORM

I. FEALTY

A man who finds nothing but prevarication
in the sing-speak of the faithful,
not strained certainty in the fervent love of the ascetic,
nor doubt in the guileful adoration of the falsely contrite,
not well-disposed visions, the illumination,
the Spirit of the Most Beneficent, the Most Merciful
nor the propensity for the enactment of the adiamorphic—
devoid of power, such a man came before my sight.

Blessed was this apostate, in earthly circumstance,
but for all the opulence that surrounded him,
he felt chilled to his very inner marrow,
and his eyes, once a lovely shade of wonder,
were dull and gaunt for witnessing malevolence,
abhorrent atrocities committed in the name of whim
by men comparable in fame and legacy to the Pharaohs,
them like the ancient kings had cast out this wanderer.

Chased by the semblance of a bird of ill-omen,
his dreary eyes, so full of confusion and regret,
took in my countenance and the humble cloth
in which I was attired, coverings which could scarcely hide
the awakened intensity within me—his senses stole when
provoked into utter observance (they sought to abet
the revival of his floundered belief), a path,
and spent he installed himself at my side.

Drawn, he reached in daring to touch
the dark mark of subjugation centered upon my forehead,
an abrasion wrought of meticulous prostration
to the fairly universal concept of an Absolute Being.
"I would steal your fealty," the traveler said, with so much
zeal that I momentarily feared him still black lead,
a failed repossession of probity, a complete negation
of the principles first impressed, urged into diffuse keeping.

Evenly, I beseeched him rest, and together we sat
facing east, feet turned away from that sacred object
before us, the rolling sands unwound, as a hot wind
buffeted our shoulders, a comfort against the cold terrain
stretched for eons in every direction—a prayer mat
placed at the verge of the crossroads to protect
supplicants such as ourselves, those who have sinned,
from balking at the prospect of kneeling before the arcane.

"Forgive me," the nomad said imploringly,
then placed his hand upon mine instead, and I joined them,
touching together the palms, despite the sanctions,
the deterrents long decreed against such fond intimacies.
"What called you here, Traveler?" I inquired kindly,
although I suspected, and professed in future to condemn
his tears, which coursed slow and sullen in fashion
down the length of his hope laden posturing like emissaries

Granted leave to inflict their own brand of misery.
"I followed," he stammered, "I followed," he professed
again, "I followed the sound."
And nodding, I acknowledged, "The steadfast truth—"

it sometimes seemed that they wrested Him from mythology,
and in my failing to accept his divinity, thrice I have stepped
away, refusing the audacity that they compound
which—"wrought my conviction in my pagan youth.

"Infancy, more like, for their voices rang
with strength and knowing, through the empty channels
of my mercurial heart, filling it to bursting,
filling it to brim, with every resounding verse
and intoned hymn, their songs and chants began
to quench an unknown thirst, though I sought to dismantle
once, the very foundation of all existence, yearning
for the capacity that lies in oblivion without remorse."

II. DISTINCTION

"I came to this life a profane essence with holes already carved
in my soul. There was snow that year, where prior was none—
perhaps," I supposed to the itinerant, "my sorrow
had infected the land.

"Our traditions were surprisingly monotheistic—we believed
in a single Creator, *Ngai*, and prayed facing Kírínyaga,
his saintly perch, the center, our *Mukurwe wa Nyagathanga*,
our Eden, where the wild fig trees grew in abundance,

and the first man, *Gikuyu*, was commanded to settle,
take *Mumbi* to wife, and where she bore him nine daughters—
*Wanjikú, Wanjirú, Wangeci, Wambúi, Wangari, Wacheera,
Waithera, Wairimú, Wangúi.*

"I was bestowed an uncommon name, not one of the nine,
for whatever came before it, brought death to whomever
it was conferred—by then, the name was generational,
and I cannot say which ancestress

first bore the distinction, they died readily in those days,
before the colonials came, bringing with them
their handy medicines and even more handy guns—
and so to break that fatal hold,

a new appellate rose from the ashes of the old.
But for the sing-speak of the faithful, I would have learned
to pray facing Kírínyaga—and Sinai would have been Sinai,
nothing more than a rock, nothing more than a place

from which moralistic myth abounds.
But Father rinsed me, and so baptized, in my sixth year,
I embraced the Eastern Orthodoxy, that brand of Catholicism,
I latched on to it wholeheartedly and for years to come

judged my immortal soul
by precepts that were sung
in languages
I didn't understand."

III. BELIEF

"When the burden
of my womanhood came
into full bloom,
I tired of the hypocrisy
that seemed to swirl
endlessly
and lost faith.

"Into that willing

g
a
p

two new faiths
entered my sphere,
not simultaneously,
but still intertwined,
for they were as a
whirlwind of foreign
sights and sounds,

o the sounds—
which distinguished themselves so profoundly
that they penetrated the murk of my adolescent season,
a season marked by angry delight
with a world surely forgotten of kindness.
I still hear that bell, which tolled for hours
beyond possible belief, that incantation absconded
with the intoner's every mortal failing...
Idolatry!—was all I could think, listening intently
through the bedroom door, locked away
as she was from the intrusive world;

in those brief moments—and in between them,
it would seem like days had passed,
as if in the space of those hours,
galaxies had condensed into existence and perished—,

in those brief moments, when we would venture
into that haven of tempting renewal,
bearing food in offering to both the minstrel
and the spirits her sing-speak was meant to supplicate,

I glimpsed
prayer beads
wrapped
comfortably about
her palms,
the bell,
a bowl really
and one of several,
some full,

some devoid,
which held
with tranquility
a liquid sanctity,
still,
wayfarer,
I thought it
nothing,
a spectacle.

'What does she do with the fruit?' I queried of her daughter
        and the girl returned, so simply, 'She eats it.'
        I knew myself then.
A heretic fool."

IV. Appeal

"In my life, I gained and lost belief
a number of times, thrice forwards and back again
to stand before the altar of that rocky temple.

It was the sing-speak of the faithful that tore me away,
and the sing-speak of the faithful
that will keep me in the straight way.

Years passed, *has the indigent state been so long
in commanding?*—and I have come to conclude
it was the stark and driven sound

of Nichiren's chant

which did not appeal,
for I found the Byzantine sounds

that engaged me to the ecumenical
in that of the 'The Teaching of the Elders,'
and as surely as I know my own name,

—birthed of ash and to dust I will return—
I know it is that thread of sounds
which brought me to the will and imperfect obedience.

And in my life, I gained and lost belief
a number of times, thrice forwards and back again
to stand before the altar of that rocky temple.

It was the sing-speak of the faithful that tore me away,
and the sing-speak of the faithful
that will keep me in the straight way."

BEYOND REDEMPTION

They stand and sit in judgment, poised
upon the spare arms of Justice,
with all the earthly grace circumstance—
and more often than not choice—denied them;
full grown perhaps, so that their chords might function
to form wellsprings of intelligent disparagement,
speech which they will use to engage at large
the court of Hosts, the veracity that shall damn me.

I can hardly deny their claims,
all I've ever wanted is to sell my pain to the world,
that I may know my suffering was never made in vain,
but in embracing my changeling humanity,
a steadfast acquaintance with morality escaped me.
That knowledge is mine now, however,
and though you may know it, I shall not speak it;
instead, might I inject this bit of inanity,
like what the title Frost/Nixon brings to mind:

It leads me to wonder if winter never graced
the White House lawn at any other time,
and if not, what blankets it in lieu of snow
when blackbird cold flaps its merry wings?

Is it shreds of classified
"FOR EYES OTHER THAN MINE ONLY"
documents,

which then like the Red Queen's inattentive landscapers,

Secret Service agents have to paint green in the dead of night
when the spring season threatens so that none might be the wiser?

But I'm rambling, and besides,
envy of State secrets is a wasted pursuit—
I have my own arcane truths, equally admissible,
which shall tip the weighted scales,
to more than allow hellfire to lick deliciously,
to flay me to skin to bone to bare teeth...

Come full circle haven't I?

O, and William, might I just say,
"Love is not Time's wasted fool if love is love of self."
"And what of harbingers of self-destruction," you ask,
"who tempt love into sin and leave love to sin?"
In perfect cynicism, I reply, "Lust, and not love,
is she who is Time's weary companion.

"Love is that which has carved its marks indelibly into my skin,
marks which delineate nurture's worn casing, a cask housed
beneath concave literature that nestled the sweetly ignorant
in nurture's same weary sac. No, lust
is she who has forged those who stand and sit in judgment,
who roamed the vale of my dreams, a precognitive warning,
whose eyes will bear into mine when the trumpet sounds,
and in that final day they will find me beyond redemption."

HOW TO DISPEL SACRED IMAGES IN A HANDY PINCH

Stand before your printer, which, like a Greyhound
is tensed to spring after the rabid ink it can't tone,

milk crate fat as it has become, as wide of girth as
that black chain link fence which each year becomes

as insurmountable as a god finger, Everest I think
He calls it in His spare time, or is it Etna or St. Helens?

Eventually, it will erupt in the way of microphones
when carbon Doo-wop breath is breathed over them,

already it shadows Cleopatra's Needle, though what of
that tale is believable anyway, "The Bull of Victory?"

Certainly, Horus is more like soap, a dry read in need of
        refreshment,
a good soaking to mend his caked and broken body,

so like that Valentine's Day monkey who hates adoration
whose tinny whine rebuffs while it also entreats, "Show me the
        love."

ORDER, IN THE CAST OF STILL SHADOWS

Need flows, *staccato* beats, a jazzy trumpet piece,
through the vault like chambers of my mournful heart,

which in turn sings of its despair in a quivering contralto,
notes sustained longer than their normal duration,

a ballad that bemoans the lack of symmetry,
the lack of a mode of proper arrangement,

the poor state of affairs my house is in,
a sorrowful telling of my desire for order.

Fear of inefficacy grips me in relentless measures,
a composition played *forte*, and gasping, overwhelmed,

the *crescendo* drives unmercifully home the substantiate:
I am steward to two of the next generation—

son and daughter of vivacious spirit—
and they require a solid foundation to build their intentions.

But while fear is a masterfully written piece
that resonates throughout, chiming fervent prisms

about that pulsing enclosure of crimson and ivory,
determination flounders, rarely heard or felt

beyond the threshold of my inner sanctum,
a place I frequently visit and stand before my reflection;

in critical manner, I often bleat at myself sharp reviews,
often scathing remarks, yet structure continues to elude me.

What now shall I do, what more can I do?
Sacrifice must come again in great number

for rewards that are as grains of sand,
insignificant when they are but a few.

The time will come however, when I am an indomitable sound,
a *concerto* of unwavering movements, a definitive mark

a willfully soaring spirit survived of the cast of still shadows,
ribbons of dark matter that fetter it to the waste of an unforgiving
        past.

SPECTER

Argent light shines down upon a grave dappled hill.
Death does not walk here, instead it sleeps,

though, upon rare occasions when
the earth's satellite seeks reprieve,

behind billows of sky-bound veils stained cerise,
the Sandman's sway knows a brief surcease,

and phantasms conceived of Platonic philosophy,

shadows cast against the light in the stance of foes,
rise from their crypts—

displace not earth, not air,
distort and make false semblance,

lay claim to continued existence,
illusory.

FATHER, OVER THE LONG YEARS

I struggle, Father, with the conclusion of your account,
for most times, when my eyes opened
upon dreadful way stations, skin stretched tight

over a belly rounded by new life,
hope seemed like forgotten lore—a tale told
upon dreadful way stations, skin stretched tight.

I vaguely remember those early years, still
as they were from perpetual fears, I will
struggle, Father, with the conclusion of your account,

when most times, my eyes open
longing for days spent in the company of eternal dreamers,
where hope proves to glimpse itself surprisingly resilient,

no predetermined finale, for believers carry it with them
unto planes intangible to mortal flesh—though
I struggle, Father, with the conclusion of your account,

hope will be born and reborn, seeds sown by fertile nature
upon this the realm of our existence, but know
I struggle, Father, with the conclusion of your account,
upon dreadful way stations, skin stretched tight.

THE SWEETS AND THE SOUR

why must there come always
the sour with the sweets?

bitter aftertaste—
settle on the tongue,
cling to the back of the throat,
and choke me while

the meadowlark bills
sixpence a sacrifice,
dues for the repose—

harsh,

the lies of fools.
life is as the fairy tales
that sang us to sleep,
happy ever afters that we in turn
pass on to hope—

all the while, remain
forever as babes,
never learning the tart
flavors of despair,
never knowing how gladly
joy is chased by sorrow.

TOWARD GLORY, BURNING

The tender pith toils in a tide of insidious thirst,

light flares, paper burns crisply,
leafy contents send acrid smoke trailing lazily skyward,
and contentment swells starved lungs denied their usual fill.

The eons swallow empty hands whole,

infinitum, immortalibus, immutable craving in my terminable coil!
Bedlam reigns, reverberant zeal then flourishes,
pugnacious, pummeling, pounding despondency

into line, for dependency

does not suit me.
I cannot bring myself to belong amongst this lot,
I will never refrain from striving toward glory.

SIXPENCE FOR SACRIFICE

"Sing a song of sixpence a pocket full of rye ..." ~ Nursery Rhyme

Sing a song of salvation, an ode to the rightful guide,
six and twenty years it took the meadowlark to confide.
A tale of discovery to impart the understanding,
has the Indigent State been so long in commanding?
In my land, sorrow rains down as thick as honey,
while wishes stream upward, imploring for days sunny;
but shadows cast against the light in the stance of foes—
the meadowlark bills sixpence a sacrifice, Dues for the Repose.

*For information regarding featured readings and general
author appearances, please visit our website.*

www.urbancentigrade.com

www.ingramcontent.com/pod-product-compliance
Lightning Source LLC
Chambersburg PA
CBHW031633040426
42452CB00007B/807